CHAMPION CRACKUPS

MORE THAN 140 SENSATIONAL SPORTS JOKES

Text copyright © 2008 by Kingfisher
KINGFISHER
Published in the United States by Kingfisher, an imprint of Henry Holt and Company LLC,
175 Fifth Avenue, New York, New York 10010. First published in Great Britain by Kingfisher
Publications plc, an imprint of Macmillan's Children's Books, London.

Distributed in Canada by H. B. Fenn and Company Ltd.

Library of Congress Cataloging-in-Publication-Data
has been applied for.

ISBN: 978-0-7534-6208-9

Kingfisher books are available for special promotions and premiums.
For details contact: Director of Special Markets, Holtzbrinck Publishers.

First Paperback American Edition June 2008
Printed in India
10 9 8 7 6 5 4 3 2 1
1TR/0208/THOM(PICA)/80STORA/C

CHAMPION CRACKUPS

MORE THAN 140 SENSATIONAL SPORTS JOKES

Illustrated by Gary Swift

KINGFISHER
NEW YORK

How do you start a Jell-O race?
Say, "Get set!"

What's a vampire's favorite sport?
Skin diving.

What happens when a sailboat gets old?
It keels over.

**Who won the
milk-drinking contest?**
*The cat. It lapped
the field.*

**Why did the potato
go to the game?**
*So that it could root
for the home team.*

**What type of
child can jump
higher than
a house?**
*All types. Houses
can't jump!*

WHO NEEDS BRAINS?

A coach walked into the locker room before a game, looked over at his star player, and said, "I'm not supposed to let you play since you failed math, but we need you in there. So, I'm going to ask you a math question, and if you get it right, you can play."

The player agreed, so the coach looked intently into his eyes and asked, "Okay, now concentrate hard and tell me the answer to this: what is two plus two?"

The player thought for a moment and then answered, "Four?"

"Did you say *four*?" the coach exclaimed, excited that he had gotten it right.

Suddenly, all of the other players on the team began screaming . . .

"Come on, Coach, give him another chance!"

A faucet, a head of lettuce, and a tomato were having a race . . . what happened?
The faucet was running, the lettuce was ahead, and the tomato was trying to ketchup!

What did the bumblebee striker say?
"Hive scored!"

Susie: I went riding last weekend.
Sarah: Horseback?
Susie: Yes, the horse got back around two hours before I did!

Knock Knock!
Who's there?
General Lee.
General Lee who?
Generally, I go to
practice, but today
I have a game.

How do you stop
squirrels from
playing ball games
in the yard?
Hide the ball; it
drives them nuts.

What did one
baseball say
to the other?
"I'm outta here!"

Rachel went out for a ride on her pony. When she returned home, she was covered in mud.

"What happened?" asked her mom.

"Well," said Rachel, "you know where the path forks at the edge of town? Well, my pony wanted to go to the right, and I wanted to go to the left."

"So what did you do?" asked her mom.

"We flipped for it, and I lost!" said Rachel.

Why don't grasshoppers go to soccer games? *They prefer cricket matches!*

Why did Cinderella get kicked off the baseball team?
She ran away from the ball.

What type of tea do soccer players drink?
Penaltea!

What's a sailor's favorite snack?
Chocolate ship cookies.

Which insect isn't a very good goalie? *A fumblebee!*

Knock Knock!
Who's there?
Canoe.
Canoe who?
Canoe come out and play today?

Why should you be careful when playing against a team of big cats? *They might be cheetahs!*

What type of
leather makes the
best ice-hockey skates?
*I don't know, but banana
peels make the best slippers!*

What type of
horses do monsters
use for racing?
Nightmares.

Where does a sailor go when
his sail gets a hole in it?
To the wholesale store.

How do you stop
moles from digging
up football fields?
Hide their shovels.

What is Count Dracula's
favorite sport?
Bat-minton!

How can you swim
one mile in just a
few seconds?
Go over a waterfall.

JUST HORSING AROUND

Three racehorses were standing in a stable bragging to each other one day. The first horse boasted, "I've run fifty-nine races, and I've won thirty-five of them."

"That's nothing," said the second horse. "I've raced ninety-seven times, and I've won seventy-eight!"

The third horse joined in, "Well, I've raced one hundred and twenty-two times, and I've won one hundred and two!"

Just then, the horses heard a voice say, "I've beat all of you!" The horses looked down and saw a greyhound. "I've raced more than two hundred times, and I've NEVER lost!"

The horses looked at the dog in amazement. Then one of them said, "How about that! A talking dog!"

**What did the
tennis ball say
when it got hit?**
*Who's making all
that racket?*

**What did the
world's worst
athlete do?**
*Ran a bath and
came in second.*

**Why is a football
stadium always cold?**
Because it's full of fans!

LET'S HEAR IT FOR THE CENTIPEDE!

There was a big soccer game between the jungle animals and the creepy-crawlies. The creepy-crawlies were one player down, and the jungle animals were winning easily. At halftime, the creepy-crawlies' coach made a passionate speech to rally them.

At the start of the second half the jungle animals had the ball but the creepy-crawlies soon starting getting the better of them. There was a penalty because the elephant was caught diving. Then the rhino got sent off for arguing with the referee. Then there was a free kick because the hippo was offside. At the end of the game the creepy-crawlies were tied with the jungle animals.

The coach rallied his players again before extra time. "Who made the elephant dive?" he asked.

"I did," said the centipede. "I tripped him!"

"Who rattled the rhino?"

"Uh, that was me, too," said the centipede. "I called him a 'snorter.'"

"And what about the hippo? Who made him go offside?"

"Well, that was me too," said the centipede. "When I kicked the ball away."

"So where were you during the first half?" demanded the coach.

"Well," explained the centipede, "I was lacing up my cleats!"

What's green,
red, and yellow and
wears boxing gloves?
Fruit punch!

Why did the
chicken get sent
out of the game?
*For persistent
fowl play.*

What helps ghosts
win games?
Their team spirit!

What's a sailor's favorite food?
Navel oranges.

How long does it take to learn how to ice-skate?
A few sittings.

How does an octopus go out onto the baseball diamond?
Well armed!

A YUCKY ICE-FISHING STORY

Two men had been sitting out on a lake all day long ice fishing. One had been having no luck at all, and the other had been pulling fish after fish out of his hole in the ice. The man having no luck finally leaned over and asked the other man what his secret was.

"*Mmmmm mmm mm mmmm mmm mmmm mmm.*"

"I'm sorry—what did you say?"

"*Mmmmm mmm mm mmmm mmm mmmm mmm.*"

"I'm sorry—I still don't understand you."

The successful man spat something into his hand and said, "You've got to keep your worms warm."

What is a golfer's favorite letter?

T.

What lives underwater and swims 100 miles per hour?

A motor pike.

A coach was being interviewed after he had resigned from a soccer team.

"Weren't the crowd behind you?" asked the reporter.

"They were right behind me, all right," said the coach, **"but I managed to shake them off at the bus station!"**

Jack was sent home from school to get his gym clothes for PE. When he got back to school, he was soaking wet.

"What happened to you?" asked his teacher.

"You told me I had to wear my gym clothes for PE," replied Jack, "but they were in the wash!"

Why can't two elephants go swimming?
Because they only have one pair of trunks!

What do you call a very intelligent tennis player?
A racket scientist.

Why did the baseball smell?
Because it hit a foul ball!

What did the inflatable coach say to the inflatable rower who was caught holding a pin on the inflatable boat?
"You let me down, you let your team down, and you let your school down, but most of all, you let yourself down."

Where do ghosts go swimming?
In the Dead Sea.

Why didn't the dog want to play tennis?
It was a boxer!

What do you call a girl who stands between two goalposts?
Annette.

Sam said to his friend, "I'm not going to play golf with Jim anymore. He cheats."

"Why do you say that?" asked his friend.

"Well, he found his lost ball two feet from the green."

"That's possible."

"Not when I had it in my pocket!"

Parent 1: What position does your child play on the team?
Parent 2: I think he's one of the drawbacks!

Coach: I'll give you one hundred dollars a week to start with and two hundred dollars a week in one year's time.

Young player: Okay, I'll come back in one year's time!

When is a basketball player like a baby?
When she dribbles!

Why did the golfer wear two pairs of pants?
In case he got a hole in one.

Why don't karate experts salute? *They might hurt their heads!*

A BIZARRE BICYCLING STORY

By the time they reached the top of a steep hill, two riders on a tandem bicycle were panting and sweating profusely.

"Phew, that was a tough climb," said the rider at the back.

"You're not kidding," replied the rider at the front. "It was a good thing I kept the brakes on, or else we would have slid back down the hill."

What position did the two ducks play on the soccer team?
Right and left quack.

Harbormaster: There's no fishing allowed here.

Boy: I'm not fishing. I'm teaching my pet maggot how to swim!

What did the left soccer cleat say to the right soccer cleat?
"Between us we should have a ball."

IQ TEST FOR SOCCER PLAYERS

1. What language is spoken in France?

2. Write an essay on the ancient Babylonian Empire, with particular reference to architecture, literature, law, and social conditions. Or give the first name of JAMES Bond.

3. Did William Shakespeare:
   (a) build a bridge
   (b) sail the ocean
   (c) lead an army
   (d) WRITE A PLAY

4. What time is it when the big hand is on the 12 and the little hand is on the one?

5. Spell: CAT, DOG, and PIG.

6. Six kings of England have been named George, the last one being George the Sixth. Name the previous five.

EXTRA CREDIT:
Using your fingers, count from one to five.

SILLY SPORTS BOOKS

How to Race Politely *by Hugo First*

The Winning Streak *by I. M. A. Winner*

Soccer Disasters *by Owen Goal*

Winter Sports for Softies *by Kay Ping-Warm*

Downhill Skiing *by Bunny Slope*

Guide to Fishing *by Captain Hook*

Anyone for Tennis? *by Nettie Racket*

Who Says I'm a Sore Loser?
by I. Sulk

How to Slam Dunk by Ima Giant

Keep on Going by U. Ken Dewitt

How to Improve Your Bowling by X. Strike

Enjoy Swimming by Di Ving-Bord

Baseball Beginners by Fursten Base

Snorkeling for Fun by Bubbles Galore

Exercise for Hamsters by Ona Wheel

Motor Racing for Beginners by Stall Dowt

Student: I've thought of a way to make the school team better.
Teacher: Great! Are you leaving it?

What happened when Santa Claus took boxing lessons?
He decked the halls!

Jane: Did you hear the joke about the rope?
Katie: No.
Jane: Oh, skip it!

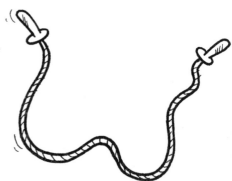

Jack: You've got holes in your basketball shorts.

Ben: No I don't!

Jack: Then how do you get your legs in them?

What's the best day for sailing?

Winds-day!

Jason's baseball team was trying to get to the top of the Little League.

"I'm sure we can do it," said Jason. "We just need to win eight of our next four games!"

Why isn't it safe to make jokes when you're ice-skating?
Because the ice might crack up!

What is usually found up a golfer's nose?
A bogey in the hole.

What do elephants play in a car?
Squash.

It had been raining heavily all week, and the soccer field resembled a swamp. However, the referee ruled that play was possible and tossed the coin to determine ends.

The away team won the toss, and after a moment's thought the coach said, "We'll take the shallow end!"

Where does Superman go bowling? *At Lois Lanes.*

Why can't two waiters play tennis?
They only want to serve!

Two boys were having their first cricket lesson.

"How do you hold the bat?" one asked.

"By the wings, of course," replied the other.

Ms. Lyle's class was doing warm-ups in the gym. "Next," said the PE teacher, "lie down on your backs and bend and stretch your legs in the air as if you were riding a bicycle."

A few seconds later she asked, "Ginny, why aren't you pedaling?"

"I'm freewheeling, Ms. Lyle!"

Why did Frankenstein stop boxing?
He didn't want to ruin his good looks!

A DIPPY DIVER

A diver was enjoying the underwater world. He saw someone at the same depth as him, wearing no scuba gear whatsoever.

The diver went down another ten feet, and the other person joined him a minute later. The diver went even deeper, and shortly after, the same person joined him.

This confused the diver, so he took out a waterproof chalkboard and wrote, "How can you stay this deep without any breathing equipment?"

The other person took the board and chalk and wrote, "I'm drowning, you moron!"

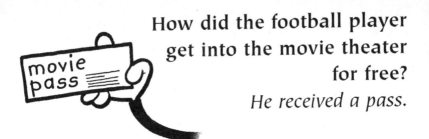

How did the football player get into the movie theater for free?

He received a pass.

Why did the dinghy sailor always carry a bag of dried fruit with her?

So that if she got into difficulty, the currants would carry her ashore.

Why was Bart Simpson kicked off the baseball team?

For hitting a Homer!

Claire: The teacher said I could play on the school soccer team if it wasn't for two things.
Jo: What are they?
Claire: My feet!

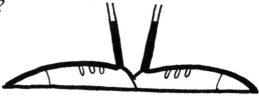

Why did the man in the kayak take a squirt gun with him?
So that he could shoot the rapids!

What do sailors like in their soup?
Crew-tons.

Two ice skaters were having a race.

As one passed the other, she said, "Guess who's going to come first?"

"Not you," said the one she was passing, "because you're skating on thin ice!"

"Sorry I missed that goal," said Josh to his coach. "I could kick myself."

"Don't even try," said the coach. "You'd miss!"

Alex: My dog plays tennis.
Tom: *He must be very smart.*
Alex: He's not that smart—I almost always win!

Neighbor 1: How do you like our new swimming pool?
Neighbor 2: *It's great, but why isn't there any water in it?*
Neighbor 1: We can't swim!

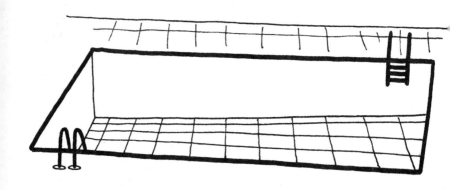

What did the fisherman take home from the game?
The catch of the day.

How short can tennis shorts be?
They're always above two feet!

Coach: Our new midfielder cost ten million dollars. I call him our wonder player.
Fan: Why's that?
Coach: Every time he plays, I wonder why I bothered to hire him!

What do you get if you cross a racecar with a computer?
Something that can crash at 200 miles per hour!

Why did the cricket team hire a cook?
They needed a good batter.

Rosie and Mike were having a great time in the snow.

"You can borrow my sled if you want to," said Mike.

"Thanks," said Rosie. **"Let's take turns."**

"Okay," said Mike. *"I'll have it going downhill, and you can have it going uphill!"*

Why did Tarzan spend so much time on the golf course?
He was perfecting his swing!

What's the hardest thing about learning how to ride a horse?
The ground!

How do elephants dive into swimming pools?
Headfirst.

Why was the snowman hopeless at playing in important games?
He always got cold feet.

What has 12 legs and two wings?
A hockey team.

Did you hear about the boy who tried to swim across the lake? When he was halfway to the other side, he decided that he was too tired, so he turned around and swam back again!

What do athletes do when they're not running?
Surf the Sprinternet!

Why did the high jumper check the calendar?
To see if it was a leap year.

Did you hear about the two fathers who ran in the parents' race on sports day?
One ran in short bursts, and the other ran in burst shorts!

How many golfers does it take to change a light bulb?
Fore!

Did you hear about the boxing referee who used to work at a rocket-launching site?
If a fighter was knocked down, he'd count: ten, nine, eight, seven . . .

Fred showed up for the Olympic Games with some barbed wire under his arm. He won the bronze medal in fencing.

Why did the runner bring his barber to the race?
He wanted to shave a few seconds off his time.

When is a swimsuit like a bell?
When you wring it out!

What do you call a boxer who gets beaten up in a fight?
A sore loser!

A little girl watching a water-skier said to her father, "That man is so silly. He'll never catch that boat!"

What happens to a football player when his eyesight starts to fail. *He becomes a referee!*

Why do elephants wear tennis shoes? *For tennis, of course.*

What race is never run?
A swimming race.

Coach: Twenty teams in the league, and you all finish at the bottom!
Team captain: Well, it could have been worse.
Coach: How?
Team captain: There could have been more teams in the league!

My brother's a professional boxer.
Heavyweight?
No, featherweight. He tickles his opponents!

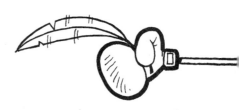

"I caught a twenty-pound salmon last week."
"Were there any witnesses?"
"There sure were. If there hadn't been, it would have been forty pounds."

What do a pool table and a coat have in common?
They both have pockets!

What has 22 legs and goes, "Crunch, crunch, crunch?"
A soccer team eating potato chips.

After his horse lost the race, the owner was furious. "I thought I told you to make a rush at the end!" he screamed at the jockey.

"I would have," answered the jockey, "but I didn't want to leave the horse behind."

What has 18 legs and catches flies?
A baseball team.

What can you serve but not eat?
A tennis ball!

What are Brazilian
fans called?
Brazil nuts!

What type of cats
like to go bowling?
Alley cats.

I wanted to have a career in sports, but
I had to give up the idea. I'm under six
feet tall, so I couldn't play basketball.
I'm only 190 pounds, so I couldn't play
football, and I have 20/20 vision, so I
couldn't be a referee.

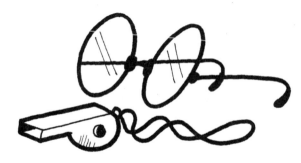

What does the winner of a race lose?
His breath!

Knock Knock!
Who's there?
Willy.
Willy who?
Willy score?
Bet he won't!

Why are football stadiums odd?
Because you can sit in the stands, but you can't stand in the sits!

SEE YOU LATER, ALLIGATOR

While fishing off the coast of Florida, a tourist capsized his boat. He could swim, but his fear of alligators kept him clinging to the overturned craft. Spotting an old beachcomber standing on the shore, the tourist shouted, "Are there any alligators around here?"

"Nah!" the man hollered back. "They ain't been around for years!"

Feeling safe, the tourist started calmly swimming toward the shore. Around halfway there, he asked the man, "How'd you get rid of the alligators?"

"We didn't do nothin'," the beachcomber said. "The sharks got 'em."

Why did the basketball player throw the basketball into the water?
Because his coach told him to sink it!

Why was the skeleton always left out in judo?
Because he had no body to go with.

What does it mean when you see 11 elephants wearing pink shirts?
They're all playing for the same team!

A GOOFY GOLF STORY

Once there was a golfer whose drive landed on an anthill. Rather than move the ball, he decided to hit it where it lay. He gave a mighty swing. Clouds of dirt and sand and ants exploded from the spot—everything but the golf ball. It sat in the same spot.

The golfer lined up and tried another shot. Clouds of dirt and sand and ants went flying again. The golf ball didn't move.

Two ants survived. One dazed ant said to the other, "Whoa! What are we going to do?"

The other ant said, "I don't know about you, but I'm going to get on that ball!"

Why did the soccerball leave the team?
It was tired of being kicked around!

Knock Knock!
Who's there?
Caddy.
Caddy who?
Caddy your own clubs!

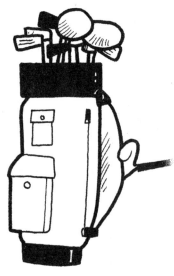

Why is a tennis match so loud?
Because the players raise a racket!

What's the quietest sport? *Bowling—you can hear a pin drop!*

Why can't a bicycle stand up? *Because it's two-tired.*

Coach: I thought I told you to lose some weight. What happened to your three-week diet? *Player: I finished it in three days!*

**What is the best part of
a boxer's joke?**
The punch line!

**Rebecca: Were you any
good at running when
you were at school, Dad?**
*Dad: Well, I once ran
a mile in less than four
minutes. And if I ever find
out who put those ants in
my pants, I'll get him!*

**Mom: Did you get
into another fight at
the game today?
You've lost your
front teeth.**
*Son: No, I haven't—
they're in my pocket.*

What did the bowling ball say to the bowling pins?
Don't stop me; I'm on a roll!

How do hens encourage their favorite teams?
They egg them on.

Why can't bad actors fish?
Because they always forget their lines.

WOULDN'T IT BE FUNNY IF . . .

A tennis player needed a match?
A fighter needed a box for his ring?
A fisherman saw Annette?
A quarterback passed out?
A golfer joined a club?
A jockey felt hoarse?
A surfer waved?